Ace Your Ma...

GEOMETRY

W9-AJS-071

3 4028 07920 0888
HARRIS COUNTY PUBLIC LIBRARY

J 516 Win
Wingard-Nelson, Rebecca
Geometry

$9.95
ocn707486589
01/24/2012

Ace your Math Test

Rebecca
Wingard-Nelson

Enslow Publishers, Inc.
40 Industrial Road
Box 398
Berkeley Heights, NJ 07922
USA

http://www.enslow.com

Library of Congress Cataloging-in-Publication Data

Wingard-Nelson, Rebecca.
  Geometry / Rebecca Wingard-Nelson.
      p. cm. — (Ace your math test)
  Summary: "Re-inforce in-class geometry skills such as lines, angles, polygons, triangles and the Pythagorean theorem"— Provided by publisher.
  Includes index.
  ISBN 978-0-7660-3783-0
  1. Geometry—Juvenile literature. I. Title.
  QA445.5.W5545 2011
  516—dc22
                                          2011006225
Paperback ISBN 978-1-4644-0010-0
ePUB ISBN 978-1-4645-0455-6
PDF ISBN 978-1-4646-0455-3

Printed in the United States of America

092011 Lake Book Manufacturing, Inc., Melrose Park, IL

10 9 8 7 6 5 4 3 2 1

To Our Readers: We have done our best to make sure all Internet Addresses in this book were active and appropriate when we went to press. However, the author and the publisher have no control over and assume no liability for the material available on those Internet sites or on other Web sites they may link to. Any comments or suggestions can be sent by e-mail to comments@enslow.com or to the address on the back cover.

♻ Enslow Publishers, Inc., is committed to printing our books on recycled paper. The paper in every book contains 10% to 30% post-consumer waste (PCW). The cover board on the outside of each book contains 100% PCW. Our goal is to do our part to help young people and the environment too!

Illustration Credits: Shutterstock.com

Cover Photos: © iStockphoto.com/Derek Latta

CONTENTS

Test-Taking Tips

Be Prepared!

Most of the topics that are found on math tests are taught in the classroom. Paying attention in class, taking good notes, and keeping up with your homework are the best ways to be prepared for tests.

Practice

Use test preparation materials, such as flash cards and timed worksheets, to practice your basic math skills. Take practice tests. They show the kinds of items that will be on the actual test. They can show you what areas you understand, and what areas you need more practice in.

Test Day!

The Night Before

Relax. Eat a good meal. Go to bed early enough to get a good night's sleep. Don't cram on new material! Review the material you know is going to be on the test.

Get what you need ready. Sharpen your pencils, set out things like erasers, a calculator, and any extra materials, like books, protractors, tissues, or cough drops.

The Big Day

Get up early enough to eat breakfast and not have to hurry. Wear something that is comfortable and makes you feel good. Listen to your favorite music.

Get to school and class on time. Stay calm. Stay positive.

Test Time!

Before you begin, take a deep breath. Focus on the test, not the people or things around you. Remind yourself to do your best and not worry about what you do not know.

Work through the entire test, but don't spend too much time on any one problem. Don't rush, but move quickly, answering all of the questions you can do easily. Go back a second time and answer the questions that take more time.

Read each question completely. Read all the answer choices. Eliminate answers that are obviously wrong. Read word problems carefully, and decide what the problem is asking.

Check each answer to make sure it is reasonable. Estimate numbers to see if your answer makes sense.

Concentrate on the test. Stay focused. If your attention starts to wander, take a short break. Breathe. Relax. Refocus. Don't get upset if you can't answer a question. Mark it, then come back to it later.

When you finish, look back over the entire test. Are all of the questions answered? Check as many problems as you can. Look at your calculations and make sure you have the same answer on the blank as you do on your worksheet.

Let's Go!

Three common types of test problems are covered in this book: Multiple Choice, Show Your Work, and Explain Your Answer. Tips on how to solve each, as well as common errors to avoid, are also presented. Knowing what to expect on a test and what is expected of you will have you ready to ace every math test you take.

1. Basic Terms

Points

A point is an exact location. Points have no length or width. A point may be thought of as a dot on a piece of paper.

What point is shown in red?

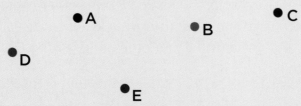

Step 1: Find the red point. The capital letter next to the point, B, names the point. In geometry, points are normally named by a capital letter.

Point B is shown in red.

Lines

A line is a straight set of points that travel in two directions without end. Lines can be thought of as the straight lines that can be drawn with a ruler on a piece of paper. Arrows are used to show that the line extends in both directions forever.

TEST TIME: Multiple Choice

Which of the following is NOT a way to name the line shown?

        a. Line RS
        b. Line f
        c. Line Rf
        d. $\overleftrightarrow{SR}$

Lines can be named by any two points on the line. Answer a uses the word *line* and two points. Answer d uses the symbol for line and two points. Both of these are correct. A line can also be named using a lowercase letter. Answer b uses the lowercase letter *f*. Answer c is not a correct way to name a line.

Solution: The correct answer is c.

Test-Taking Hint

Multiple choice questions give you a set of answers. You choose which of the given answers is correct.

Definitions

line segment: Part of a line with two endpoints.

ray: Part of a line that starts at one endpoint and
extends without end in one direction.

plane: A flat surface that extends in all directions
without end.

Line Segments

*Name three line segments that have point B as one
endpoint.*

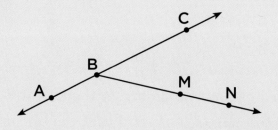

Step 1: Line segments are named using two endpoints in any
order. The symbol for a line segment is similar to that for a
line, but it has no arrow. The segment that has endpoints at
point A and B can be named $\overline{AB}$ or $\overline{BA}$.

Choose any three segments that have point B as an endpoint.

$\overline{AB}$, $\overline{BC}$, and $\overline{BM}$

TEST TIME: Show Your Work

Draw a figure that includes line LX and ray XY.

Each person who draws this figure may have a different looking answer. Some problems can have different answers and still be correct. In this problem, line LX and ray XY share point X.

Draw line LX to begin.

A ray is named using the endpoint first and then any other point on the ray. Ray XY, or $\overrightarrow{XY}$, has an endpoint at point X, then extends forever in a direction that goes through point Y. Draw a point Y, and extend a ray through it.

Test-Taking Hint

Questions that do not give you solutions to choose from are sometimes called "Show Your Work" questions. You may need to fill in a blank, make a drawing or graph, or show the equations or work that you used to find your answer.

Definitions

intersecting lines: Lines that meet or cross.

point of intersection: The place where two lines or line
segments meet.

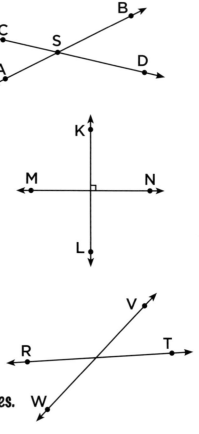

Lines AB and CD are
intersecting lines.
The point of intersection
is point S.

perpendicular lines: Intersecting
lines in the same plane that
form right (90°) angles.
The symbol ⊥ means "is
perpendicular to."
$$\overleftrightarrow{KL} \perp \overleftrightarrow{MN}$$

oblique lines: Intersecting lines
in the same plane that do
not form right (90°) angles.
Lines RT and VW are oblique lines.

TEST TIME: Multiple Choice

Which two lines are perpendicular?

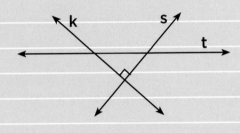

    a. Lines k and s   **b.** Lines s and t

    c. Lines k and t   **d.** None of them

Perpendicular lines form right angles. These are sometimes called square corners. There are four square corners where lines k and s intersect.

Solution: The correct answer is a.

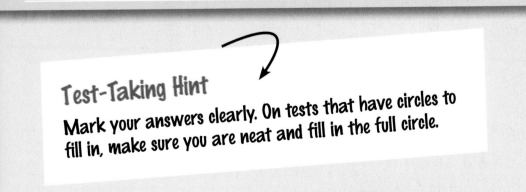

Test-Taking Hint

Mark your answers clearly. On tests that have circles to fill in, make sure you are neat and fill in the full circle.

Definition

parallel lines: Lines in the same plane that never intersect. Parallel lines are always the same distance apart. The symbol ‖ means "is parallel to."

Line r ‖ line s

r ←————————————→

s ←————————————→

Skew

Will the orange lines ever cross? How are they related?

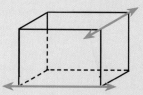

Step 1: Answer the first question. Will the orange lines ever cross? If the lines are extended forever in both directions, will they cross?

No, the orange lines will never cross.

Step 2: Answer the next question. How are the lines related? Are they in the same plane? Imagine a flat surface like a table top. Can one flat surface contain both of these orange lines? No. The lines are in different planes. Lines that do not cross and are in different planes are called skew. (Lines that never cross and are in the same plane are parallel.)

The orange lines are skew.

TEST TIME: Explain Your Answer

Lines a, b, and m lie in the same
plane. Line a is parallel to line b.
Line m is perpendicular to line a. Explain how line m and
line b are related.

Solution:

When two lines are parallel and a third line is perpendicular
to one of the lines, then it is also perpendicular to the second
of the two lines. Line a and line b are parallel. Line m is
perpendicular to line a, so it is also perpendicular to line b.

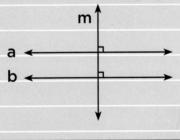

Test-Taking Hint

Some problems ask a question and ask you to explain your answer.
Others just ask for an explanation. Your score is based on both a
correct response and how clearly you explain your reasoning. If there
is no direct computation, try to include an example when you can.

Definitions

angle: A figure formed by two lines or rays with a common endpoint. Angles are named using the angle symbol, ∠.

vertex: The corner point in a geometric figure. In an angle, the vertex is the common endpoint. The vertex of ∠ABC is point B.

Intersecting Lines

How many angles are formed when two lines intersect? What do all of the angles have in common?

Step 1: Use a diagram to understand and answer the problem.
Draw two intersecting lines.

Step 2: Count the angles.

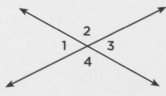

There are four angles.
They each have the same vertex.

TEST TIME: Multiple Choice

Which of the following is the correct way to name the angle?

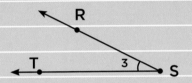

a. ∠RST

b. ∠S

c. ∠3

d. all of the above

Angles are named in three ways: using the vertex, using three letters with the vertex at the center, or using a number that is inside the angle.

Solution: Since answers a, b, and c are all correct, the correct choice is answer d, all of the above.

Test-Taking Hint

In multiple choice problems with the answer choice all of the above, it is best to check all of the choices.

Definition

angle measurement: The measure of an angle tells how far one edge of the angle is turned from the other. The most common measurement unit for angles is degrees. The symbol for degrees is °.

acute angle: An angle with a measure that is less than 90°.

45°

right angle: An angle with a measure that is exactly 90°.

90°

obtuse angle: An angle with a measure that is greater than 90°, but less than 180°.

135°

straight angle: An angle with a measure that is exactly 180°.

180°

Angle Names

Classify each of the following angles by their measure.

1

2

3

∠1 is a
right angle.

∠2 is an
obtuse angle.

∠3 is a
straight angle.

TEST TIME: Explain Your Answer

Define and draw an example of an acute angle.

Solution: Acute angles have a measure that is less than 90°.

A 90° angle is like the corner of a paper. Draw an angle that is smaller than the corner of a paper.

Test-Taking Hint
Knowing math definitions helps you understand what the problem is asking.

4. Angle Relationships

Definitions

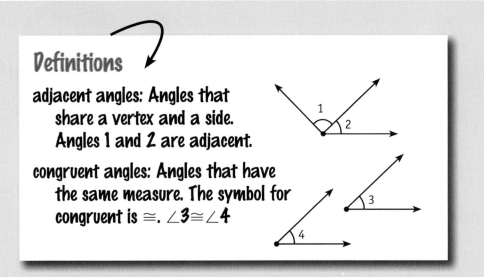

adjacent angles: Angles that share a vertex and a side. Angles 1 and 2 are adjacent.

congruent angles: Angles that have the same measure. The symbol for congruent is ≅. ∠3≅∠4

Congruent Angles

Angles 3 and 5 are congruent. What is the measure of 5?

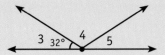

Step 1: What is the measure you are given in the diagram?

$$m\angle 3 = 32°$$

Step 2: Congruent angles have the same measure. When you know the measure of one angle, you also know the measure of the other. You know the measure of ∠3, so you know the measure of ∠5.

$$m\angle 5 = 32°$$

When a question is taking an especially long time, or has you stumped, leave the question and go on. Come back later if you have time. Another question may give you a clue that can help you solve the problem.

TEST TIME: Show Your Work

Name an angle adjacent to ∠STQ.

Adjacent angles share a vertex.
The vertex of ∠STQ is point T.

Adjacent angles share a side.
The sides of ∠STQ are $\vec{TS}$ and $\vec{TQ}$.
There are two angles shown that share
a vertex and a side with ∠STQ. The
adjacent angle must be named using three points with the vertex in the center.

Solution: Angles STR and QTU are both adjacent to ∠STQ.

Angle Sums

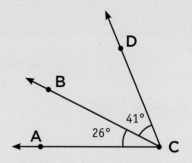

What is the measure of ∠ACD?

Step 1: You are given the measure of ∠ACB and ∠BCD.

m∠ACB = 26°
m∠BCD = 41°

Step 2: You can add the measures of angles that share sides to find the measure of the combined angle.

m∠ACB + m∠BCD = m∠ACD
  26° +   41°   =   67°

m∠ACD = 67°

Definitions

complementary angles: Two angles that have measures with a sum of 90°. Complementary angles form a right angle when they are adjacent.

supplementary angles: Two angles that have measures with a sum of 180°. Supplementary angles form a straight angle when they are adjacent.

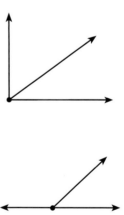

TEST TIME: Multiple Choice

Which pair of angles is complementary?

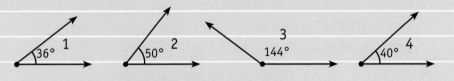

        a. *1 and 2*

        b. *1 and 3*

        c. *2 and 3*

        d. *2 and 4*

Complementary angles have a sum of 90°.

The measures of $\angle 2$ and $\angle 4$ have a sum of 90°.

Solution: The correct choice is answer d.

Test-Taking Hint

Some of the answers may look correct if you do not read the questions carefully. In the question above, you could easily choose answer b if you confuse complementary and supplementary.

5. Intersecting Lines

Definitions

linear pair: Two adjacent angles
formed when lines intersect.
Linear pairs are always
supplementary.

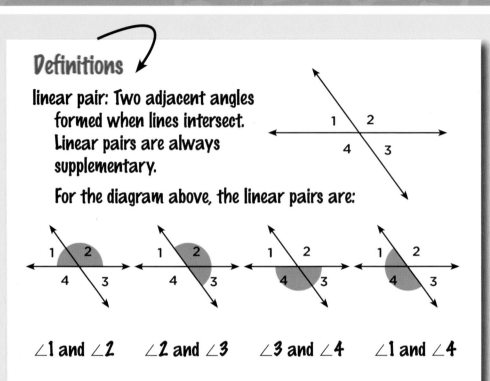

For the diagram above, the linear pairs are:

∠1 and ∠2   ∠2 and ∠3   ∠3 and ∠4   ∠1 and ∠4

vertical angles: Two angles that are NOT adjacent when two
lines intersect. Vertical angles are always congruent.

For the diagram above, the vertical angles are:

∠1 and ∠3   ∠2 and ∠4

TEST TIME: Multiple Choice

What is the measure of ∠3?

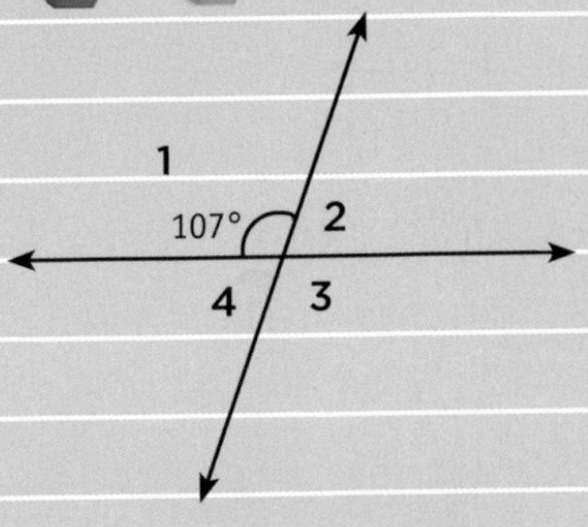

a. 17°

b. 73°

(c.) 107°

d. 124°

The diagram gives the measure of ∠1. Angles 1 and 3 are vertical angles. Vertical angles are congruent. Congruent angles have the same measure. This means ∠1 and ∠3 have the same measure, 107°.

Solution: The correct answer is c.

Test-Taking Hint

Put a small mark next to answers you're not sure of or do not finish. When you finish your test, go back to those problems.

TEST TIME: Show Your Work

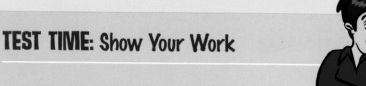

What is the measure of ∠PRQ?

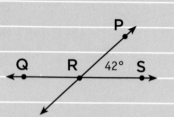

Angles PRQ and PRS are a linear pair. Linear pairs are supplementary. Their sum is always 180°.

You know the sum of the two angles, and you know the measure of one of the angles. You can use subtraction to find the measure of the other angle.

Solution:
$$m\angle PRQ + m\angle PRS = 180°, \text{ so}$$
$$180° - m\angle PRS = m\angle PRQ$$
$$180° - 42° = m\angle PRQ$$
$$180° - 42° = 138°$$

$$m\angle PRQ = 138°$$

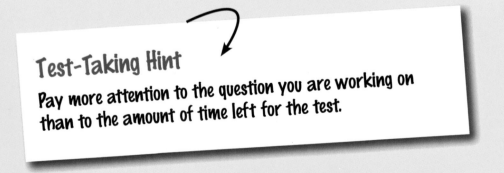

Test-Taking Hint

Pay more attention to the question you are working on than to the amount of time left for the test.

Complete Circle

The measure of angle 1 is 18°.
Find the measure of ∠2, ∠3,
and ∠4. What is the sum of
all four angles?

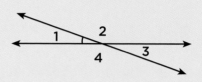

Step 1: Angles 1 and 2 are a linear pair. Find the measure of angle 2 by subtracting the measure of angle 1 from 180°.

180° − 18° = 162°
The measure of ∠2 is 162°.

Step 2: Angles 1 and 3 are vertical angles. Vertical angles are congruent. The measure of angle 3 is the same as the measure of angle 1.

The measure of ∠3 is 18°.

Step 3: Angles 2 and 4 are vertical angles. Vertical angles are congruent. The measure of angle 4 is the same as the measure of angle 2.

The measure of ∠4 is 162°.

Step 4: Add the measure of the four angles.

18° + 162° + 18° + 162° = 360°

An angle that goes the entire way around a circle measures 360°.

Definitions

transversal: A line that intersects at least two other lines.

corresponding angles: A pair of angles in matching corners when a transversal intersects parallel lines. Angles 1 and 5 are corresponding angles.

alternate interior angles: A pair of angles inside parallel lines and on opposite sides of a transversal. Angles 3 and 6 are alternate interior angles.

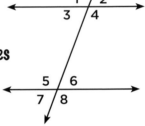

alternate exterior angles: A pair of angles outside parallel lines and on opposite sides of a transversal. Angles 1 and 8 are alternate exterior angles.

Corresponding Angles

Find the measure of ∠6.

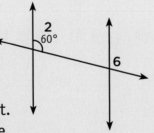

Step 1: Angles 2 and 6 are corresponding angles. Corresponding angles are congruent. When you know the measure of one, you also know the measure of the other.

m∠6 = 60°

TEST TIME: Multiple Choice

How are angles 3 and 6 related?

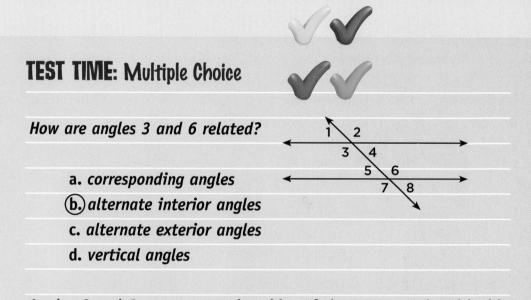

   a. corresponding angles
   b. alternate interior angles
   c. alternate exterior angles
   d. vertical angles

Angles 3 and 6 are on opposite sides of the transversal and inside the two parallel lines. They are alternate interior angles.

Solution: Answer b is correct.

Test-Taking Hint

An answer in a multiple choice problem might look correct if you go too quickly. Often the wrong answers listed are ones you would find if you made a common error.

Congruent Angles

Given: $\overleftrightarrow{m} \parallel \overleftrightarrow{n}$ and $m\angle 5 = 50°$.

Which angles have a measure of 50°?
Give a reason for each.

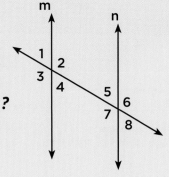

Step 1: Some problems give you
information in both the problem and
a diagram. This problem tells you that lines m and n are
parallel. It also tells you that the measure of $\angle 5$ is 50°.

$m\angle 5 = 50°$ **This is given.**

Step 2: Vertical angles are congruent. Angles 5 and 8 are
vertical angles.

$m\angle 8 = 50°$ **(vertical angles)**

Step 3: Alternate interior angles of two parallel lines crossed
by a transversal are congruent. Angles 4 and 5 are alternate
interior angles.

$m\angle 4 = 50°$ **(alternate interior angles)**

Step 4: Alternate exterior angles of two parallel lines crossed
by a transversal are congruent. Angles 1 and 8 are alternate
exterior angles.

$m\angle 1 = 50°$ **(alternate exterior angles)**

Angles 1, 4, 5, and 8 each measure 50°.

TEST TIME: Explain Your Answer

When two parallel lines are crossed by a transversal, what is the relationship between the consecutive interior angles? Explain your reasoning.

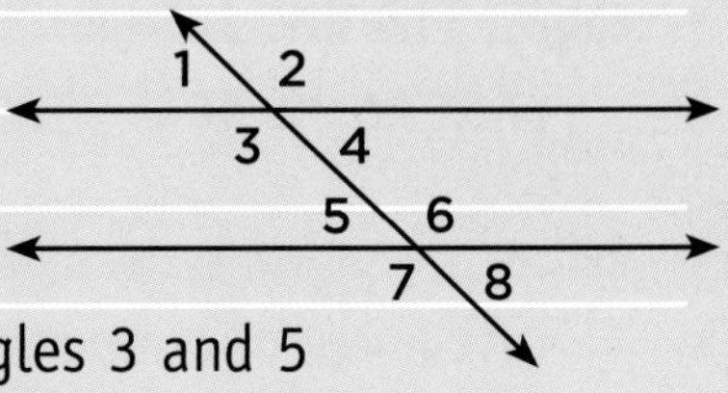

Solution: Consecutive interior angles are a pair of angles that are on the same side of a transversal and inside the parallel lines. Angles 4 and 6 and angles 3 and 5 are consectutive interior angles. Let's look at angles 4 and 6.

Angles 4 and 5 are congruent because they are alternate interior angles. This means they have the same measure.

Angles 5 and 6 are supplementary because they are a linear pair. Their sum is 180°.

Since angles 4 and 5 have the same measure, angles 4 and 6 must also have a sum of 180°, which means they are supplementary.

Consecutive interior angles are also called same side interior angles. Same side exterior angles, such as angles 2 and 8 in the diagram, are also supplementary.

7. Polygons

Definitions

plane figure: A set of connected line segments and curves that lie in one plane.

edges: The line segments or curves that make up a plane figure.

vertex: A point where line segments or curves of a figure meet. The plural of vertex is vertices.

closed figure: A plane figure that has no end points.

open figure: A plane figure that has a beginning and ending point.

polygon: A closed plane figure with edges that are all line segments.

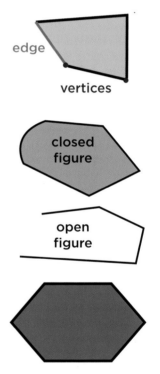

edge

vertices

closed figure

open figure

TEST TIME: Show Your Work

Which of the following appear to be regular polygons?

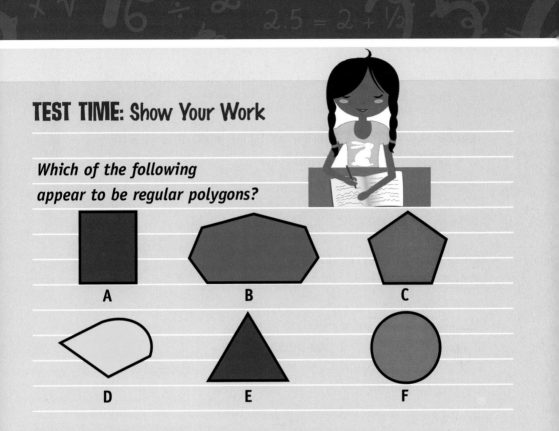

Regular polygons have congruent sides and angles. Each side is the same length. Each angle has the same measure.

Figure A is taller than it is wide.

Figure B has one very long side.

Figure C appears to be regular.

Figure D is not a polygon, because one edge is a curve.

Figure E appears to be regular.

Figure F is not a polygon.

Solution: Figures C and E appear to be regular polygons.

Definitions

convex polygon: A polygon with all interior angles less than 180°.

concave polygon: A polygon with at least one interior angle greater than 180°.

Convex or Concave

Is the polygon at right convex or concave?

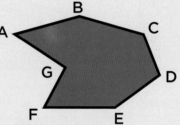

One way: There are a number of ways to decide if a polygon is convex or concave. Look at each angle inside the polygon. Are any of them greater than 180°? Yes. The angle inside the polygon at vertex G is greater than 180°. This polygon is concave.

Second way: When a vertex appears to point into the polygon, the polygon is concave. Vertex G appears to point into the polygon, so the polygon is concave.

Third way: In a convex polygon, any line segments drawn between two vertices (diagonals) are inside the polygon. When a diagonal is not inside the polygon, the polygon is concave. A diagonal from point A to point F is outside the polygon, so the polygon is concave.

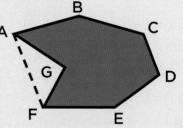

The polygon is concave.

TEST TIME: Multiple Choice

*Name the shape of
the given polygon.*

        a. triangle
        b. pentagon
        c. heptagon
        d. octagon

Polygons are named by the number of sides and angles they have. Some polygon names are easily recognized, like triangle and rectangle. Others can be figured out by applying what you know about other words. For example, an octagon has 8 sides, just as an octopus has 8 tentacles.

Count the number of sides. There are 7. You know a triangle has 3 sides, so a is not correct. An octagon has 8 sides, so answer d is not correct. It is likely that you will also recognize that a pentagon has 5 sides. This leaves only answer c. A heptagon has 7 sides.

Solution: Answer c is correct.

Test-Taking Hint

Common prefixes can help you remember the number of sides on a polygon. Such as tri- means 3, quad- means 4, and penta- means 5.

Definition

triangle: A three-sided polygon. Triangles have three
angles and three vertices.

Naming Triangles

Name the red triangle.

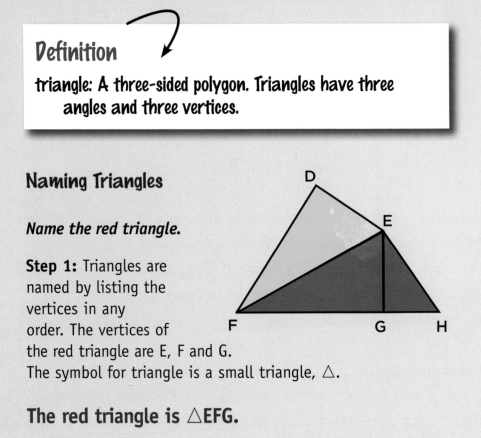

Step 1: Triangles are
named by listing the
vertices in any
order. The vertices of
the red triangle are E, F and G.
The symbol for triangle is a small triangle, △.

The red triangle is △EFG.

Test-Taking Hint

Word problems, or story problems, should be answered in
complete sentences.

TEST TIME: Show Your Work

Sean has three pipe cleaners.
The lengths are 8 inches, 5 inches,
and 4 inches. Can Sean make a triangle from the three
pipe cleaners?

For any three lengths to form a triangle, the sum of the shorter
two lengths must be greater than the longest length. Add the
two shortest lengths and compare the sum to the longest.

Solution:

The two shortest pipe cleaners are 5 inches and 4 inches.
5 inches + 4 inches = 9 inches

The longest pipe cleaner is 8 inches.
Is 9 inches greater than 8 inches? Yes.

Yes, Sean can make a triangle using the three pipe cleaners.

Definitions

acute triangle: A triangle with three angles less than 90°.

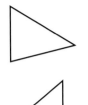

right triangle: A triangle with one 90° angle.

obtuse triangle: A triangle with one angle greater than 90°.

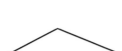

equilateral triangle: A triangle with three congruent sides. Equilateral triangles are also equiangular. They have three congruent angles.

isosceles triangle: A triangle with exactly two congruent sides.

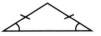

scalene triangle: A triangle with no congruent sides.

Test-Taking Hint

Small hatch marks and arcs are used to show that sides or angles are congruent.

Test-Taking Hint

Knowing the names of angles (acute, right, and obtuse) will help you remember the names of triangles.

TEST TIME: Multiple Choice

Classify △ABC by angle measure and by side length.

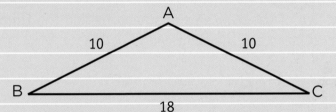

a. △ABC is a right scalene triangle.

b. △ABC is an obtuse scalene triangle.

c. △ABC is an acute isosceles triangle.

d. △ABC is an obtuse isosceles triangle.

Look at the angles of triangle ABC. Angles B and C are acute. Angle A is obtuse. Triangle ABC is obtuse.

Look at the sides of triangle ABC. Two sides have the same length. They are congruent. Triangle ABC is isosceles.

Solution: Answer d is correct.

Interior Angles

The interior angles of a triangle always have a sum of 180°.

What is the measure of the interior angle at vertex Y? Check your answer.

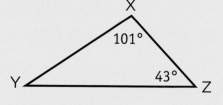

Step 1: The sum of the three interior angles is 180°.
You know two of the measures and need to find the third. Add the two measures that you know.

$$101° + 43° = 144°$$

Step 2: Subtract the sum of the two angles from 180°.

$$180° - 144° = 36°$$

The measure of the interior angle at vertex Y is 36°.

Step 3: Check your answer by adding the three angles.

$$101° + 43° + 36° = 180°$$

TEST TIME: Multiple Choice

Use mental math to find the third angle in a triangle where two of the angles each measure 50°.

> a. 50°
> b. 60°
> c. 80°
> d. 100°

Think: The interior angles of a triangle have a sum of 180°.
You know two of the angles are 50° and 50°. Add these mentally.
$$50° + 50° = 100°$$
Subtract the sum, 100°, from 180° mentally. $180° - 100° = 80°$

Solution: The correct answer is c.

Test-Taking Hint

When you can solve a problem mentally, do it and move quickly to the next problem. However, do not move too quickly! You could misread the problem.

TEST TIME: Show Your Work

What are the measures of the angles in an isosceles right triangle?

Use the definition of an isoceles right triangle and the sum of the interior angles to solve this problem.

A right triangle has one right angle, so one angle is 90°.

An isosceles triangle has two angles that are congruent, or have the same measure.

Subtract the measure of the right triangle and divide the remaining degrees by two to find the measure of the remaining two angles.

Solution: $180° - 90° = 90°$
$90° \div 2 = 45°$

The measures of the angles in an isosceles right triangle are 90°, 45°, and 45°.

Test-Taking Hint

Showing your work and showing some effort can earn you part of the credit, even if you have the wrong answer. The right answer, without showing some work, may only give you partial credit.

TEST TIME: Explain Your Answer

Can an obtuse triangle have a right angle? Explain.

Solution:

An obtuse triangle can never have a right angle.

An obtuse triangle has one angle that is greater than 90°.
The sum of all three interior angles is 180°.

If you subtract more than 90° (the obtuse angle) from 180°, you are left with less than 90° for the sum of the remaining two angles.

Therefore, each of the remaining angles must be less than 90°.

10. The Pythagorean Theorem

Definition

exponent: A value placed above and to the right of an expression that tells the number of times the expression is used as a factor. For example, 5^3 means $5 \times 5 \times 5$. Exponents are also called powers. The expression 5^3 is read as "5 to the third power."

The exponent 2 is often read as "squared," so a^2 is read as "a squared." The exponent 3 is often read as cubed, so b^3 is read as "b cubed."

Powers

Evaluate 2^4.

Step 1: The word evaluate means "find the value of." The exponent 4 tells you to use the value 2 as a factor 4 times.

$$2 \times 2 \times 2 \times 2$$

Step 2: Multiply.

$$2 \times 2 \times 2 \times 2 = 16$$

$2^4 = 16$

Which expression has a value of 36?

a. $10^2 + 3^2$
b. $4 + 3^2$
c. $(4)(3^2)$
d. 3^3

Find the value of each expression. Evaluate exponents before doing other operations.

a. $10^2 + 3^2 = 100 + 9 = 109$
b. $4 + 3^2 = 4 + 9 = 13$
c. $(4)(3^2) = 4 \times 9 = 36$
d. $3^3 = 3 \times 3 \times 3 = 27$

Solution: Answer c is correct.

Test-Taking Hint

Incorrect answers in multiple choice problems are often ones that look correct if you were to make an error.

Pythagorean Theorem: The sum of the squares of the two leg lengths of a right triangle is equal to the square of the hypotenuse. This is usuallly written as $a^2 + b^2 = c^2$, where a and b are the leg lengths and c is the length of the hypotenuse (across from the right angle).

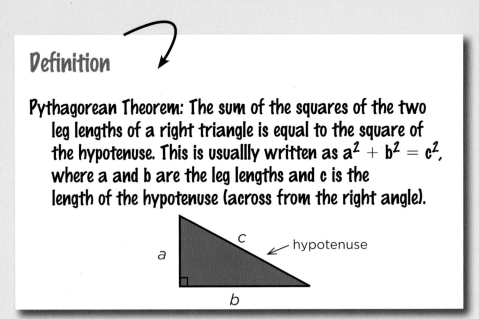

Right Angles

A triangle has sides that measure 6 inches, 8 inches, and 10 inches. Is the triangle a right triangle?

Step 1: You can use the Pythagorean Theorem to decide if a triangle is a right triangle. The longest length is always the hypotenuse. The two shortest lengths are the legs.

$$a^2 + b^2 = c^2$$
$$6^2 + 8^2 = 10^2$$

Step 2: Do the operations.

$$6^2 + 8^2 = 10^2$$
$$36 + 64 = 100$$
$$100 = 100$$

The side lengths work in the Pythagorean Theorem, so the triangle is a right triangle.

TEST TIME: Show Your Work

The legs of a right triangle are 10 feet and 24 feet. What is the length of the hypotenuse?

Substitute the values you know into the Pythagorean Theorem.

Solution:

$$a^2 + b^2 = c^2$$
$$10^2 + 24^2 = c^2$$
$$100 + 576 = c^2$$
$$676 = c^2$$

What number when multiplied by itself equals 676? 26.

$$26 = c$$

The hypotenuse is 26 feet long.

To solve a problem like this quickly and accurately, you can use a calculator for the exponents. The square root key ($\sqrt{\ }$) is used to find the number that is multiplied by itself to equal 676.

Test-Taking Hint

Calculators can be used on some tests. Use a calculator when you know how to solve a problem and it will save time you may need for other problems.

Definitions

quadrilateral: A four-sided polygon.

kite: A quadrilateral with two pairs of adjacent, congruent sides.

trapezoid: A quadrilateral with exactly one pair of parallel sides.

parallelogram: A quadrilateral with two pairs of parallel sides. The parallel sides are congruent.

rhombus: A parallelogram with four congruent sides.

rectangle: A parallelogram with four right angles.

square: A rectangle with four congruent sides.

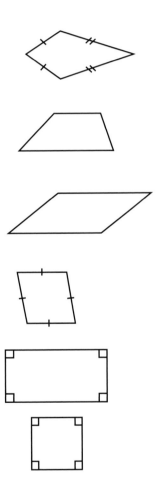

TEST TIME: Multiple Choice

What name fits the quadrilateral shown?

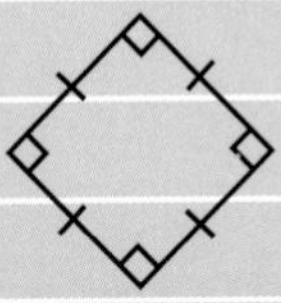

a. rectangle
b. parallelogram
c. rhombus
(d.) All of the above

The quadrilateral has two pairs of parallel sides. This makes the figure a parallelogram. It has four congruent sides. This makes it a rhombus. It also has four right angles. This makes it a rectangle. The figure can also be called a square.

Solution: The correct answer is d.

Test-Taking Hint

Not all of the questions on a math test need computations. Know math definitions and know the reasons behind the math.

TEST TIME: Explain Your Answer

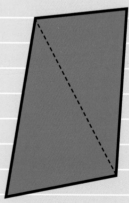

What is the sum of the interior angles of any quadrilateral? Explain your reasoning.

Solution:

To find the sum of the interior angles of a quadrilateral, divide it up into triangles. There are two triangles.

Because the sum of the angles of each triangle is 180°, you can add the angles from each triangle to find the sum of the interior angles of the quadrilateral.

180° + 180° = 360°

So, the sum of the interior angles of a quadrilateral is 360°.

Special Trapezoids

Trapezoid ABCD is an isosceles trapezoid.
What is the measure of ∠B?

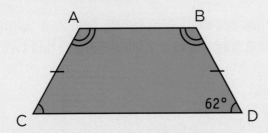

Step 1: An isosceles trapezoid is a special kind of trapezoid. Isosceles trapezoids have special properties. Opposite sides of an isosceles trapezoid are congruent. The angles on either side of the bases are congruent. Adjacent angles along the sides are supplementary.

Supplementary angles have a sum of 180°. Since the measure of ∠D is 62°, the measure of ∠B is 180° − 62°.

$$180° - 62° = 118°$$

The measure of ∠B is 118°.

Test-Taking Hint

An isosceles trapezoid is like an isosceles triangle with the top cut off parallel to the base. Even if you do not remember the properties of an isosceles trapezoid, you can solve this problem using the diagram and the sum of the interior angles.

Definition

diagonal: A line segment connecting two non-adjacent
   vertices of a polygon. Every quadrilateral has two diagonals.

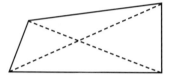

The diagonals of parallelograms bisect each other.
This means they cut each other in half.

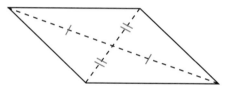

The diagonals of a rectangle form four congruent segments.

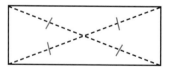

The diagonals of a rhombus are perpendicular.

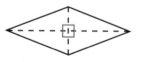

TEST TIME: Show Your Work

Quadrilateral LMOP is a rhombus.
Line segment MO is 8 centimeters long.
What is the length of line segment NO?

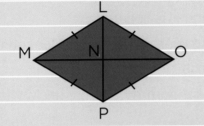

Line segment MO is a diagonal of a rhombus. A rhombus is a parallelogram, so the diagonals of a rhombus bisect each other. Line segment NO is half of line segment MO.

Solution: $8 \div 2 = 4$

Line segment NO is 4 centimeters long.

Test-Taking Hint

Remember to include the units in your answers. The units in this problem are centimeters.

TEST TIME: Explain Your Answer

The diagonals of a quadrilateral are perpendicular and form four congruent line segments. What is the most specific shape name for the quadrilateral?

Solution:

Quadrilaterals with perpendicular diagonals are rhombi. Each side of the quadrilateral is congruent.

Quadrilaterals with diagonals that form four congruent line segments are rectangles.

Quadrilaterals that are both rhombi and rectangles are squares.

The quadrilateral is a square.

Sketch a figure by drawing the diagonals first. Draw perpendicular lines that form four congruent segments. Connect the endpoints to form a quadrilateral. The figure formed is a square.

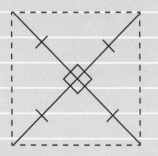

Test-Taking Hint

Use complete sentences when answering word problems and problems that ask you to explain your answer.

Using Algebra

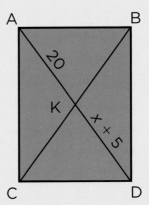

What is the value of x in the rectangle?

Step 1: Some problems combine algebra and geometry. This problem asks you to find the value of a variable, or unknown value.

The diagonals of a rectangle form four congruent line segments. This means the measures of line segments AK and KD are equal. Write this using an equal sign.

$$\text{measure of AK} = \text{measure of KD}$$

Step 2: Replace the words with the values from the diagram.

$$20 = x + 5$$

Step 3: Solve for x.

$$20 - 5 = x + 5 - 5$$
$$15 = x$$

$$x = 15$$

13. Other Polygon Angles

Interior Angle Sums

What is the sum of the interior angles of a pentagon?

Step 1: The sum of the interior angles of any polygon can be found by dividing the polygon into triangles. Each triangle has an interior angle sum of 180°. Draw a pentagon.

Step 2: Divide the pentagon into triangles by drawing diagonals from one vertex. Count the triangles.

There are 3 triangles.

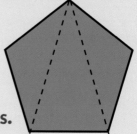

Step 3: Find the interior angle sum of the pentagon by multiplying the number of triangles (3) by 180°.

$$3 \times 180° = 540°$$

The sum of the interior angles of a pentagon is 540°.

Any polygon can be divided into triangles. Each polygon has two less triangles than it does sides. For example, a 10-sided polygon will divide into 8 triangles.

The interior angle sum for any polygon can be found by taking the number of sides minus 2 and multiplying it by 180°.

interior angle sum = (number of sides − 2) × 180°

Definition

formula: A math rule that is written using words or symbols.

TEST TIME: Multiple Choice

What is the sum of the interior angles of a polygon with 12 sides?

a. 2160°   (b.) 1800°

c. 1440°   d. 180°

Use the formula for the interior angle sums.

interior angle sum = (number of sides − 2) × 180°

$$= (12 - 2) \times 180°$$

$$= (10) \times 180°$$

You can mentally multiply any number and 10 by adding a zero on the right end.

$$(10) \times 180° = 1800°$$

Solution: The correct answer is b.

TEST TIME: Show Your Work

What is the angle measure of each interior angle in a regular hexagon?

This is a two-step problem. First, find the sum of the interior angles in a hexagon (6 sides). Then, since each angle in a regular polygon has the same measure, divide by the number of angles to find the measure of each.

Solution:

$$\text{interior angle sum of a hexagon} = (6 - 2) \times 180°$$
$$= (4) \times 180°$$
$$= 720°$$

$$\text{each interior angle of a regular hexagon} = 720° \div 6$$
$$= 120°$$

The measure of each interior angle of a regular hexagon is 120°.

Test-Taking Hint

Make sure you are answering the question that is asked. Check your answer to see that it matches the question.

Definition

central angle of a regular polygon: An angle made at the center of the polygon by the lines drawn from any two adjacent vertices of the polygon to the center. All of the central angles in one regular polygon are the same.

Central Angle Measure

What is the measure of the central angle of a regular octagon?

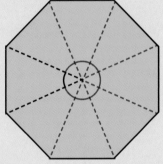

Step 1: A regular octagon has 8 congruent sides, 8 congruent interior angles, and 8 congruent central angles.

To find the measure of the central angle of a regular octagon, make a circle in the middle. A circle is 360 degrees around. Divide 360° by eight angles.

$$360° \div 8 = 45°$$

The measure of the central angle of a regular octagon is 45°.

The measure of the central angle of a regular polygon can be found by dividing 360° by the number of sides.

measure of central angle = 360° ÷ number of sides

14. Perimeter

Definition

perimeter: The distance around a figure. The capital letter P is usually used to represent perimeter in a formula.

Adding to Find Perimeter

What is the perimeter of △RST?

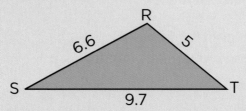

Step 1: To find the perimeter of any shape, you can add the length of all the sides.

$$6.6 + 5 + 9.7 = 21.3$$

The perimeter of △RST is 21.3 units.

Test-Taking Hint

If no units are given in a problem, you can write the answer using the word "units."

TEST TIME: Multiple Choice

What is the perimeter of a regular pentagon with side length of 2.7 centimeters?

        a. 13.5 centimeters

        b. 15.0 centimeters

        c. 17.5 centimeters

        d. 19.5 centimeters

Each side of a regular polygon has the same length. A pentagon has 5 sides, so the perimeter is found by multiplying the side length by 5.

$$2.7 \times 5 = 13.5$$

Solution: The correct answer is a.

Rectangles, Parallelograms, and Kites

What is the perimeter of the kite shown?

One way: The perimeter of any figure can be found by adding each of the sides. Kites, parallelograms, and rectangles each have two pairs of congruent sides.

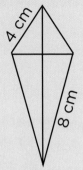

$$4 \text{ cm} + 4 \text{ cm} + 8\text{cm} + 8\text{cm} = 24 \text{ cm}$$

The perimeter of the kite is 24 centimeters.

Another way: Multiply each of the measures of the congruent sides by two. Add the products.

$$2(4 \text{ cm}) + 2(8 \text{ cm}) =$$
$$8 \text{ cm} + \quad 16 \text{ cm} = 24 \text{ cm}$$

The perimeter of the kite is 24 centimeters.

Test-Taking Hint

When you don't feel confident about an answer, and have time, try solving it a different way. That way, you are less likely to make the same mistake twice.

TEST TIME: Show Your Work

The perimeter of a rectangle is 44 meters. The width of the rectangle is 10 meters. What is the length of the rectangle?

A rectangle has 2 pairs of congruent sides. In a rectangle, these are called length and width. The perimeter of a rectangle can be found by adding 2 lengths and 2 widths. A diagram can help you to understand this problem.

Solution:

Perimeter = 2(length) + 2(width)

44 = 2(length) + 2(10)

44 = 2(length) + 20   **Subtract 20 from each side.**

24 = 2(length)   **Divide each side by 2.**

12 = length

The length of the rectangle is 12 meters.

Check: length + length + width + width = perimeter

12 meters + 12 meters + 10 meters + 10 meters = 44 meters

44 meters = 44 meters

15. Area

Definitions

square unit: A square that is one unit long and one unit wide. A square inch is one inch long and one inch wide. Square units can be written as units^2.

area: The number of square units needed to cover a figure.

Rectangles

What is the area of a rectangle that is 2 inches wide and 3 inches long?

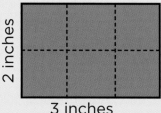

One way: Use a diagram. The diagram shows one square for each square inch. Count the number of squares. There are 6.

The area of the rectangle is 6 square inches.

Another way: Use a formula. The formula to find the area of a rectangle is length multiplied by width.

Area = length × width
Area = 2 inches × 3 inches
Area = 6 square inches

The area of the rectangle is 6 square inches.

Area Formulas

Area of a rectangle = length × width
$$A = l \times w$$

Area of a square = side × side
$$A = s^2$$

TEST TIME: Show Your Work

Brianna built a picture frame using 4 wood sides that each measure 8 inches long. Each corner is a 90° angle. She is covering it with a fabric to paint on. What is the area covered by the fabric?

Each side is the same length and the corners are 90° angles.
This picture frame is a square.
The area of a square is found by multiplying a side by itself.

Solution:

8 inches × 8 inches = 64 square inches
The area covered by fabric is 64 square inches.

Area Formulas

Area of a parallelogram = base × height

$$A = b \times h$$

Area of a trapezoid = 1/2 × (base 1 + base 2) × height

$$A = 1/2(b_1 + b_2)\, h$$

The height of a trapezoid or parallelogram is the perpendicular distance between the bases.

Parallelograms

Find the area of the parallelogram.

Step 1: Write the formula.
Put in the values from the problem.

> **Area = base × height**
> **Area = 10 × 6**

Step 2: Multiply.

Area = 60

The area of the parallelogram is 60 square units.

TEST TIME: Explain Your Answer

Use the formula for the area of a parallelogram to show why the formula for the area of a trapezoid works.

Solution:

You can double a trapezoid, flip one over, and put the two trapezoids end to end to form a parallelogram.

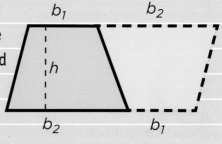

The area of this parallelogram is found using the formula.

The length of this parallelogram's base is $b_1 + b_2$.

Area of a parallelogram = base × height

Area of a parallelogram = $(b_1 + b_2)$ × h

Since this is double what the area of the trapezoid is, multiply the area of the parallelogram by 1/2 to find the area of the trapezoid.

Area of a trapezoid = $1/2(b_1 + b_2)$ × h

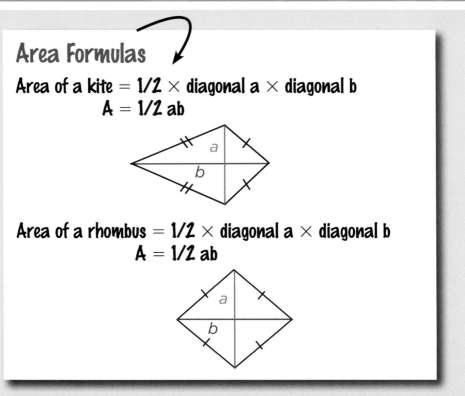

Area Formulas

Area of a kite = 1/2 × diagonal a × diagonal b
A = 1/2 ab

Area of a rhombus = 1/2 × diagonal a × diagonal b
A = 1/2 ab

Rhombus

What is the area of a rhombus with diagonal lengths of 3 feet and 2 feet?

Step 1: Write the formula. Put in the values from the problem.

Area = 1/2 × diagonal *a* × diagonal *b*
Area = 1/2(3)(2)

Step 2: Multiply.

Area = 3

The area of the rhombus is 3 square units.

TEST TIME: Multiple Choice

A kite has diagonals with lengths of 4.6 inches and 6.2 inches. What is the area of the kite?

    a. 10.8 square inches
    b. 14.26 square inches
    c. 21.6 square inches
    d. 28.52 square inches

The units in this problem are decimals. You can use a calculator to multiply decimals.

The formula for the area of a kite includes multiplying by 1/2. This is the same as multiplying by the decimal 0.5, or dividing by 2.

$$Area = 1/2(4.6)(6.2)$$
$$= (0.5)(4.6)(6.2)$$
$$= 14.26$$

Solution: The correct answer is b.

TEST TIME: Show Your Work

Bridgette wants to make a kite with an area of 102 square inches. One of the diagonals is set at one foot. How long should the other diagonal be?

The problem uses two different measurement units, inches and feet. When you perform an operation with measurement units, only use the same units. For example, only multiply inches with inches, not inches with feet.

Solution:

Area of a kite $= 1/2ab$

$102\ \text{in}^2 = 1/2(1\ \text{ft})b$	**Convert 1 foot to 12 inches.**
$102\ \text{in}^2 = 1/2(12\ \text{in})b$	**Multiply 1/2 and 12.**
$102\ \text{in}^2 = (6\ \text{in})b$	**Divide both sides by 6 in.**
$17\ \text{in} = b$	

The other diagonal should be 17 inches long.

Check:

$102\ \text{in}^2 = (1/2)(12\ \text{in})(17\ \text{in})$

$102\ \text{in}^2 = 102\ \text{in}^2$

TEST TIME: Explain Your Answer

The area formulas for a kite and a rhombus are the same. What are the differences and similarities between the diagonals in a kite and a rhombus? Could you use diagonals of the same length to form a kite and a rhombus?

Solution:

Both a kite and a rhombus have diagonals that are perpendicular at their intersection. The longer diagonal of a kite bisects the shorter. The diagonals of a rhombus bisect each other.

The same diagonal lengths can form a kite or a rhombus. If you begin with diagonals that bisect each other for a rhombus, you can slide one of the diagonals along the other to form a kite.

Area Formula

Area of a triangle = 1/2 × base × height

$$A = 1/2 \, bh$$

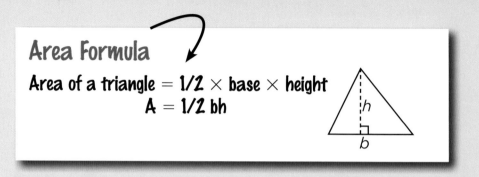

Find the Area

Find the area of a triangle with a base of 8 units and a height of 7 units.

Step 1: Write the formula.
Put in the values from the problem.

Area = 1/2 × base × height
Area = 1/2(8)(7)

Step 2: Multiply.

Area = 28

The area of the triangle is 28 square units.

Test-Taking Hint

Area is always in square units. Remember to include the units in your answer.

TEST TIME: Show Your Work

An isosceles right triangle has a leg with a length of 12 inches. What is the area of the triangle?

The height of a triangle is a perpendicular distance from the base to the opposite vertex. Any of the three sides can be the base of a triangle. If you choose one of the legs of a right triangle as the base, the other leg is the same as the height.

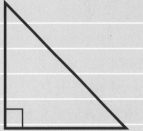

An isosceles right triangle is a right triangle with congruent legs. This makes the height and base the same length.

Solution:

$$\text{Area of a triangle} = 1/2bh$$
$$= 1/2(12)(12)$$
$$= 72$$

The area of the triangle is 72 square inches.

TEST TIME: Multiple Choice

What is the base of a triangle with an area of 1,045 square centimeters if the height is 95 centimeters?

> a. 12 centimeters
> b. 22 centimeters
> c. 200 centimeters
> d. 210 centimeters

You can use the values in the problem to find the missing value in the formula, or you can test each answer.

The formula for the area of a triangle is 1/2 base times height.

Let's say you believe answer c is correct. You can do this mentally. Area = 1/2(200)(95). Multiply 1/2 and 200 first. This leaves 100 × 95 = 9,500. This is much too large. Since answer d is larger than answer c, both can be eliminated. Test answers a and b.

a. 1/2(12)(95) = 570

b. 1/2(22)(95) = 1,045

Solution: The correct answer is b.

TEST TIME: Explain Your Answer

A student says the area of the triangle is 44 square inches. Explain why the student is incorrect.

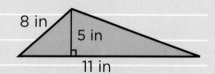

Solution:

The formula for the area of a triangle is Area = 1/2*bh*

This triangle has a base of 11 inches and a height of 5 inches.

The area is 1/2(11)(5) = 27.5 inches.

The student used the lengths of the two sides that are given, 11 inches and 8 inches, instead of base and height, 11 inches and 5 inches.

Definitions

circle: The set of all points in a plane
that are the same distance from a
given point, called the center. A circle is
named by its center. This is circle A.

chord: A line segment with endpoints
on a circle.

diameter: A chord that passes through
the center of a circle.

radius: A line segment with one endpoint
at the center of a circle and the other
at any point on the circle.

central angle of a circle: An angle
formed by two radii.

arc: Part of the curve of a circle.

sector: The part of the circle that is
enclosed by a central angle and the
arc connecting the two endpoints.

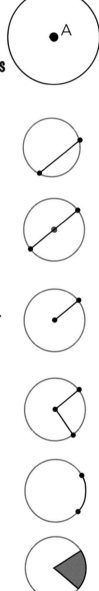

Identifying Parts

Name the parts of circle L.

a. radii

Write the radii using symbols for line segments.

$\overline{LA}$, $\overline{LB}$, $\overline{LC}$

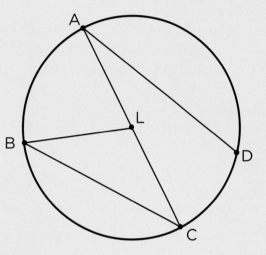

b. diameter

$\overline{AC}$

c. chords

$\overline{AC}$, $\overline{BC}$, $\overline{AD}$

d. arcs

The symbol for arc is an arch over the endpoints of the arc. If the arc is 180° or greater, include a third point.

$\overset{\frown}{AB}$, $\overset{\frown}{ABC}$, $\overset{\frown}{ACD}$

Other possible arcs:

$\overset{\frown}{BC}$, $\overset{\frown}{CD}$, $\overset{\frown}{DA}$, $\overset{\frown}{BD}$, $\overset{\frown}{CDA}$, $\overset{\frown}{DAB}$, $\overset{\frown}{BDA}$, $\overset{\frown}{CAB}$, $\overset{\frown}{DBC}$

e. central angles

$\angle ALB$, $\angle BLC$, $\angle ALC$

TEST TIME: Show Your Work

A circle graph shows the results of a survey of people and their eye color. Find the measure of the central angle of the sector that shows the percent of people with blue eyes.

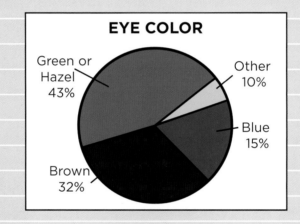

EYE COLOR

Green or Hazel 43%

Other 10%

Blue 15%

Brown 32%

The problem asks for the measure of the central angle that represents people with blue eyes. The correct answer will be an angle measure in degrees.

The sector labeled Blue is 15% of the whole circle. The central angle measure for the sector is 15% of the angle measure of the whole circle. The angle measure of a whole circle is 360°.

TEST TIME: Continued. . .

Solution:

Use the percent equation.

A percent of a whole is a part, or

percent × whole = part

Put in the values from the problem.

15% of 360° = central angle measurement

15% × 360° = central angle measurement

To multiply a percent, change the percent to a decimal.

15% = 0.15

0.15 × 360° = 54°

The central angle of the sector measures 54°.

Test-Taking Hint

When you use a calculator, you still need to understand what to do with the numbers in the problem. A calculator is only a tool, not a problem-solver.

19. Circle Measurements

Definitions

circumference: The distance around a circle.

pi: The ratio of circumference to diameter. The ratio is the same for every circle and is represented by the Greek letter π, called pi. Pi is approximately equal to 3.14 or 22/7.

Circumference

The ratio of the circumference of a circle to the diameter is π. Use algebra and this ratio to write a formula for the circumference of a circle.

Step 1: Write the ratio as an equation. Use C for circumference and d for diameter.

$$\pi = \frac{C}{d}$$

Step 2: Multiply each side of the equation by the diameter, d.

$$\pi(d) = \frac{C}{\cancel{d}}(\cancel{d}) = C$$

Step 3: Write the equation so that circumference is on the left side of the equal sign.

$$C = \pi d$$

TEST TIME: Multiple Choice

The radius of a circle is 6 inches. What is the circumference of the circle?

>   a. 3π
>   b. 6π
>   c. 12π
>   d. 24π

The circumference of a circle = π*d*. The diameter is twice as long as the radius. The formula for circumference can also be written as *C* = 2π*r*.

$$C = 2\pi r = 2\pi 6 = 12\pi$$

Solution: The correct answer is c.

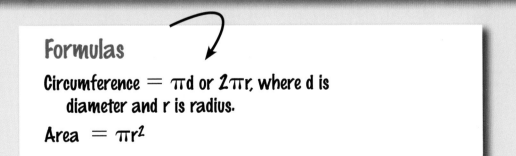

Formulas

Circumference = π*d* or 2π*r*, where d is diameter and r is radius.

Area = π*r²*

Area

Find the area of the circle to the nearest tenth. Use 3.14 for π.

3 m

Step 1: Use the formula.

$$A = \pi r^2$$

Step 2: Replace with the values from the problem. The problem tells you to use the decimal approximation for π, 3.14. When you replace π with 3.14, use ≈ instead of the equal sign. The sign ≈ means approximately.

$$A \approx (3.14)3^2$$

Step 3: Do the computations. Evaluate the power first. Then multiply.

$$A \approx (3.14)3^2$$
$$A \approx (3.14)9$$
$$A \approx 28.26$$

Step 4: Write the answer in a complete sentence. Round the area to the nearest tenth. Remember to include the units.

The area of the circle is about 28.3 m².

TEST TIME: Multiple Choice

A circular flower bed has a diameter of 28 feet. Using 22/7 as the approximation for π, what is the approximate area of the flower bed?

        a. 154 square feet
        b. 308 square feet
        c. 496 square feet
        d. 616 square feet

Use the formula. The problem gives you diameter, but the formula uses the radius. Remember, the radius is half of the diameter.
Half of 28 feet is 14 feet.

$$A = \pi r^2$$
$$A \approx (22/7)14^2$$
$$A \approx (22/7)196$$
$$A \approx 616$$

Solution: The correct answer is d.

Test-Taking Hint

Area problems for circles will often tell you what form of pi to use. Read carefully!

Polygon Combinations

What is the perimeter of the figure shown?

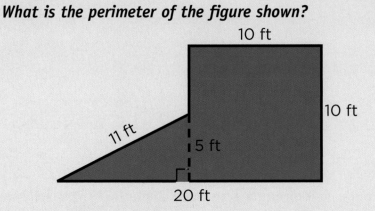

Step 1: To find the perimeter of a figure, you can add the length of each side. The length of each side is not shown, but can be found.

One section is missing. The full height of the square area is 10 feet. The triangular area is 5 feet high.

10 ft – 5 ft = 5 ft

Step 2: Add the length of each side. Choose a side to begin, and add in order around the figure.

10 ft + 10 ft + 20 ft + 11 ft + 5 ft = 56 ft

The perimeter of the figure is 56 feet.

TEST TIME: Multiple Choice

Estimate the area of the figure.
Each square represents one square foot.

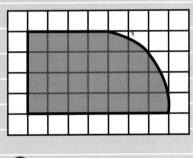

a. 25 square feet
b. 26 square feet
c. 27 square feet
d. 28 square feet

Count the number of filled or almost filled squares. There are 23.
Count the number of squares that are about half-filled. There are 4.
Add the number of filled squares and half the number of half-filled squares.

$$23 + 2 = 25$$

Solution: The correct answer is a.

TEST TIME: Show Your Work

Harrison needs to carpet his closet. The closet is rectangular, but has a raised triangular area that does not need carpet. Using the diagram, how many square feet of carpet does Harrison need?

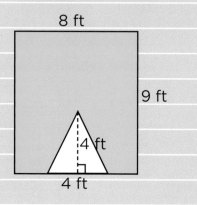

Areas that are made up of polygons like rectangles and triangles can be found by adding or subtracting the areas of the polygons they are made of.

Solution: Find the area of each figure.

Area of the rectangle = lw Area of the triangle = $1/2bh$

               = (8)(9)   = 1/2(4)(4)

               = 72   = 8

Subtract the area of the triangle from the area of the rectangle.

72 square feet − 8 square feet = 64 square feet

Harrison needs 64 square feet of carpet.

Test-Taking Hint

Most tests are scored on the number of questions you answer correctly. You do not lose points for wrong answers. Answer every question, even if you have to guess.

Using Area

The area outlined in red is a garden plot. The green-shaded area produced 3 quarts of green beans. If the entire garden is planted in green beans, about how many quarts of beans can be produced?

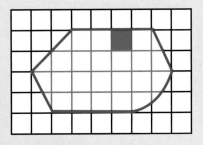

Step 1: Estimate the area inside the red outline.

> **Whole or nearly whole units: 19**
> **Half or near half units: 8**

Whole units + half of partial units: 19 + 4 = 23

Step 2: Each of the units that are planted in beans will produce about 3 quarts of beans. Multiply the number of units by 3 quarts.

23 × 3 quarts = 69 quarts

The entire garden can produce around 69 quarts of beans.

Definitions

line symmetry: A figure with line symmetry has two halves that are mirror images.

line of symmetry: The line along which a symmetrical figure is divided.

rotational symmetry: A figure with rotational symmetry can be turned around a central point less than 360° and be an exact image of itself.

center of rotation: The central point around which a figure is rotated.

Line Symmetry

Decide if each figure has line symmetry.

Figure 1: Can lines be drawn that divide the figure into mirror images? Yes.

Figure 2: No lines can be drawn to form mirror images.

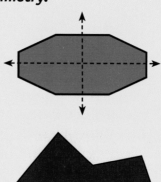

TEST TIME: Multiple Choice

How many lines of symmetry does the figure have?

a. 0
b. 2
c. 4
d. 12

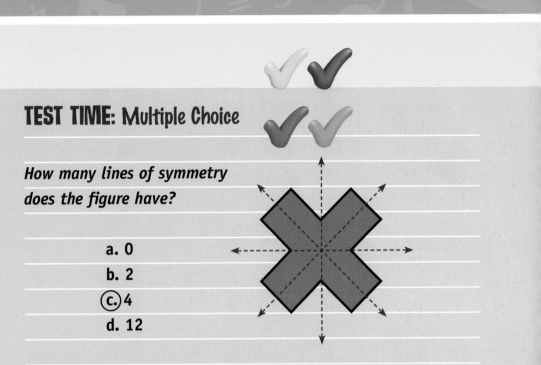

You can draw 4 lines that divide the figure into mirror images.

Solution: The correct answer is c.

Test-Taking Hint

Make notes in your test booklet to help you solve problems. For the problem above, drawing the lines of symmetry will help you see the mirror images. It will also help you count the number of lines of symmetry in the figure.

Rotational Symmetry

How many times will the figure show rotational symmetry within one full rotation?

Step 1: Draw lines from the center of the figure through identical places in the figure.

Step 2: Count the number of lines drawn.

The figure will show rotational symmetry five times within a full rotation.

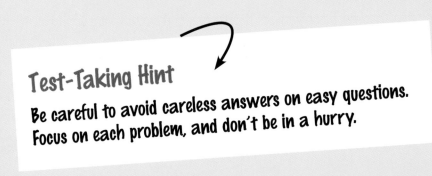

Test-Taking Hint

Be careful to avoid careless answers on easy questions. Focus on each problem, and don't be in a hurry.

TEST TIME: Explain Your Answer

What kinds of symmetry does an equilateral triangle show? Explain.

Solution:

An equilateral triangle shows both line symmetry and rotational symmetry.

Because each side and each angle of an equilateral triangle are congruent, you can draw a line of symmetry running through each vertex and the center of the opposite side.

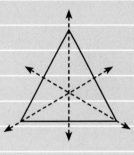

You can draw three lines from the center of the equilateral triangle through identical places in the figure. The triangle has rotational symmetry, and will show the symmetry three times within one rotation.

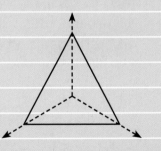

22. Similarity and Congruence

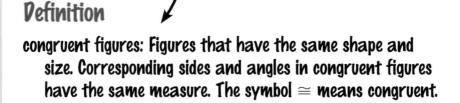

Definition

congruent figures: Figures that have the same shape and
    size. Corresponding sides and angles in congruent figures
    have the same measure. The symbol ≅ means congruent.

Compare Figures

Are the parallelograms ABCD and LMNO congruent?

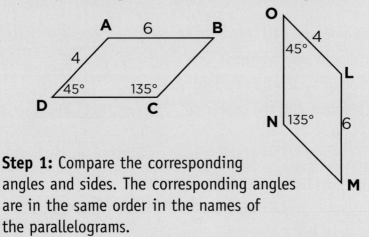

Step 1: Compare the corresponding
angles and sides. The corresponding angles
are in the same order in the names of
the parallelograms.

Corresponding angles:

∠A ≅ ∠L: 135°
∠B ≅ ∠M: 45°
∠C ≅ ∠N: 135°
∠D ≅ ∠O: 45°

Corresponding sides:

AB ≅ LM: 6
BC ≅ MN: 4
CD ≅ NO: 6
DA ≅ OL: 4

Parallelograms ABCD and LMNO are congruent.

TEST TIME: Show Your Work

Triangles ABC and XYZ are congruent.
What are the values of a and m?

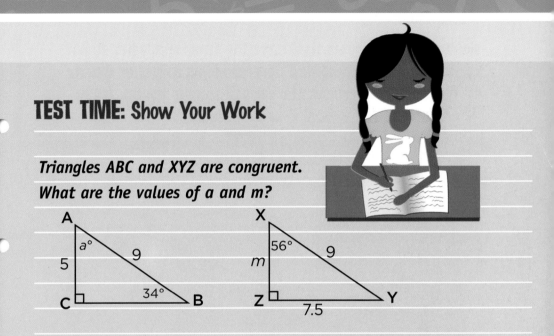

Solution:

The corresponding angles of congruent triangles are congruent.

∠A ≅ ∠X, so *a*° = 56°

The corresponding sides of congruent triangles are congruent.

AC ≅ XZ, so *m* = 5

a = 56 and *m* = 5

Test-Taking Hint

Make sure you answer the entire problem. If there are two questions, make sure you have two answers.

Definition

similar figures: Figures that have the same shape but do not need to be the same size. Corresponding angles of similar figures are congruent. The sides of similar figures are in proportion. The symbol ~ means similar.

Determine Similarity

Are the triangles similar?

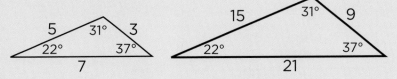

Step 1: Corresponding angles of similar figures are congruent. Are the angles congruent? Yes. Each triangle has angles that measure 31°, 37°, and 22°.

Step 2: Corresponding sides of similar figures are proportional, or have the same ratio. Write a ratio that compares each pair of corresponding sides. Reduce each ratio to lowest terms.

$$\frac{5}{15} = \frac{5 \div 5}{15 \div 5} = \frac{1}{3}$$

$$\frac{3}{9} = \frac{3 \div 3}{9 \div 3} = \frac{1}{3}$$

The corresponding sides all have the same ratio, 1 to 3. They are proportional.

$$\frac{7}{21} = \frac{7 \div 7}{21 \div 7} = \frac{1}{3}$$

Yes, the triangles are similar.

TEST TIME: Multiple Choice

The two windows shown are similar.
What is the width of the smaller window?

a. 2
b. 2.5
c. 3
d. 5

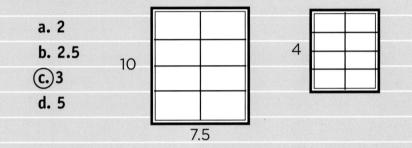

10

7.5

4

Write a proportion comparing the width and height of the windows.

$$\frac{\text{width}}{\text{height}} \qquad \frac{7.5}{10} = \frac{?}{4}$$

In proportions, the cross products are equal. Cross multiply.

$$7.5 \times 4 = 10 \times ?$$

$$30 = 10 \times ?$$

You need to find the number that can by multiplied by 10 for a product of 30. Divide 30 by 10.

$$30 \div 10 = 3$$

The smaller window is 3 units wide.

Solution: Answer c is correct.

Definitions

coordinate plane: A plane formed by a horizonal number line, called the x-axis, and a vertical number line, called the y-axis.

origin: The intersection of the x-axis and y-axis.

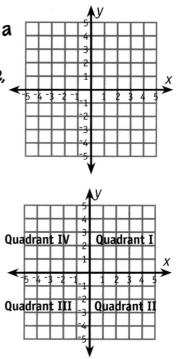

quadrants: The axes divide the coordinate plane into four regions called quadrants.

Quadrants

Identify the quadrant containing points A and B.

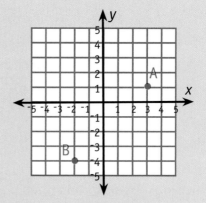

Point A: Quadrant I

Point B: Quadrant III

TEST TIME: Multiple Choice

What point is located at the ordered pair (3, 1)?

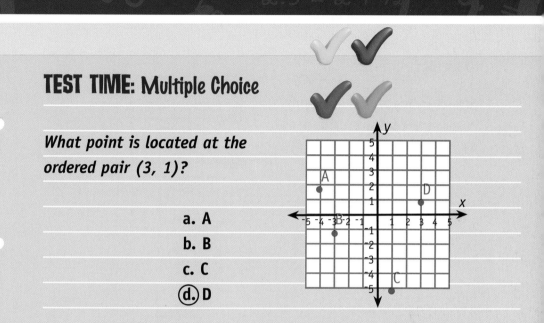

    a. A

    b. B

    c. C

    (d.) D

An ordered pair is a pair of numbers that tell the location of a point in the coordinate plane.

The first number in an ordered pair is the *x*-coordinate. It describes where on the *x*-axis the point is located, or how far the point is to the left or right of the origin. The *x*-coordinate is a positive 3. The point is 3 units right of the origin.

The second number in an ordered pair is the *y*-coordinate. It describes where on the *y*-axis the point is located, or how far the point is above or below the origin. The *y*-coordinate is positive 1. The point is 1 unit above the origin.

Point D is 3 units right and 1 unit above the origin.

Solution: Answer d is correct.

Plotting Points

Plot each point on a coordinate plane.

K(1, 4): Start at the origin. Positive *x*-values are right of the origin, negative values are left. Move 1 unit right.

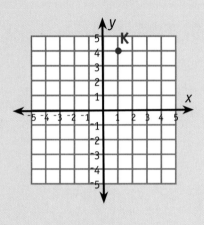

Positive *y*-values are above the origin, negative values are below. Move 4 units up.

Draw and label point K.

M(4, −2): Start at the origin. Move 4 units right and 2 units down.

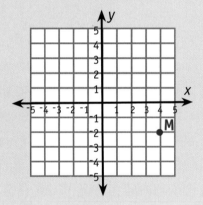

Draw and label point M.

Test-Taking Hint

You can go through a test and do the easy problems first. This can help you gain confidence, and keeps you from running out of time and missing easy points.

Test-Taking Hint

The coordinates of the origin are (0, 0).

A point with an x-value of zero is not left or right of the origin. It lies on the y-axis.

A point with a y-value of zero is not above or below the origin. The point lies on the x-axis.

TEST TIME: Explain Your Answer

To plot point (−6, −4), Kelly started at the origin and moved 6 units right and 4 units down. Is Kelly correct? Explain.

Solution:

No, Kelly is not correct. She plotted point (6,−4). Since the x-coordinate is a negative number, Kelly should have moved left from the origin instead of right.

Kelly did plot the correct y-value.

Coordinate Figures

Plot the points A(2, 3), B(2, ⁻1), C(⁻2, ⁻1), and D(⁻2, 3).
Connect the points in order and describe the figure.

Step 1: Plot each point.

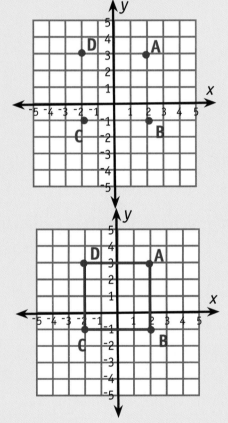

Step 2: Connect the points
beginning at A. Connect
point A to point B,
point B to point C,
point C to point D,
and point D to point A.

Step 3: Describe the figure.

The result is a figure with four equal sides and four right
angles. The figure is a square.

Definition

translation: A movement of a figure along a straight line. Translations are sometimes called slides.

TEST TIME: Multiple Choice

Point A(1, 1) is translated 2 units left and 3 units up. What are the coordinates of the new point?

    ⓐ. (⁻1, 4)
    b. (0, ⁻2)
    c. (3, 4)
    d. (⁻1, ⁻2)

Draw a sketch to help you see the movement of the point.

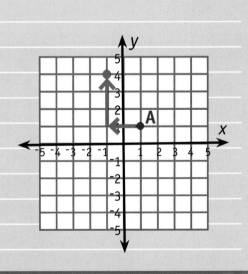

Solution: The correct answer is a.

TEST TIME: Show Your Work

Graph the translation of △PQR 4 units right and 3 units down. List the coordinates of the translated figure.

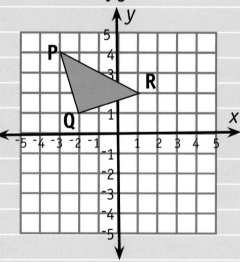

Figures are translated by translating each vertex, then connecting the translated points.

TEST TIME: Continued...

Solution:

Translate each vertex.
The vertices of a translated figure are written using the same letter with a small apostrophe ('). The new vertex is read as "prime". For example, P' is read "P prime."

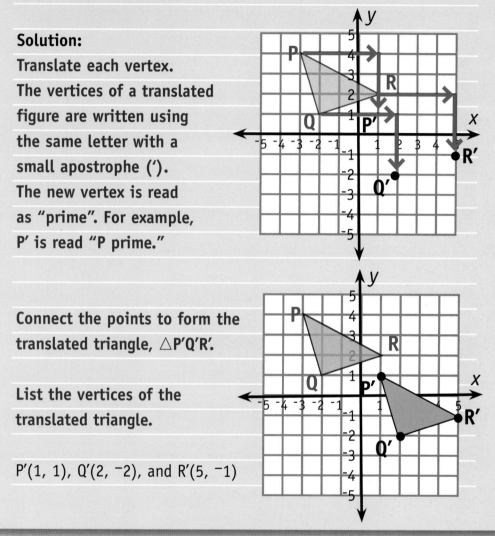

Connect the points to form the translated triangle, △P'Q'R'.

List the vertices of the translated triangle.

P'(1, 1), Q'(2, ⁻2), and R'(5, ⁻1)

Test-Taking Hint

Transformations take a figure and create an identical image. A translation is a type of transformation. Reflections (flips) and rotations (turns) are also transformations.

Further Reading

Books

Ferrell, Karen. *The Great Polygon Caper*. Hauppauge, N.Y.: Barron's Educational Series, 2008.

McKellar, Danica. *Math Doesn't Suck: How to Survive Middle School Math Without Losing Your Mind or Breaking a Nail*. New York: Hudson Street Press, 2007.

Rozakis, Laurie. *Get Test Smart!: The Ultimate Guide to Middle School Standardized Tests*. New York: Scholastic Reference, 2007.

Internet Addresses

Coolmath.com, Inc. **Geometry & Trig Reference Area.** 1997–2010. <http://www.coolmath.com/reference/geometry-trigonometry-reference.html>

Mathwarehouse.com. **Math Warehouse.** <http://www.mathwarehouse.com/geometry>

Testtakingtips.com. **Test Taking Tips.** 2003–2010. <http://www.testtakingtips.com/test/math.htm>

Index